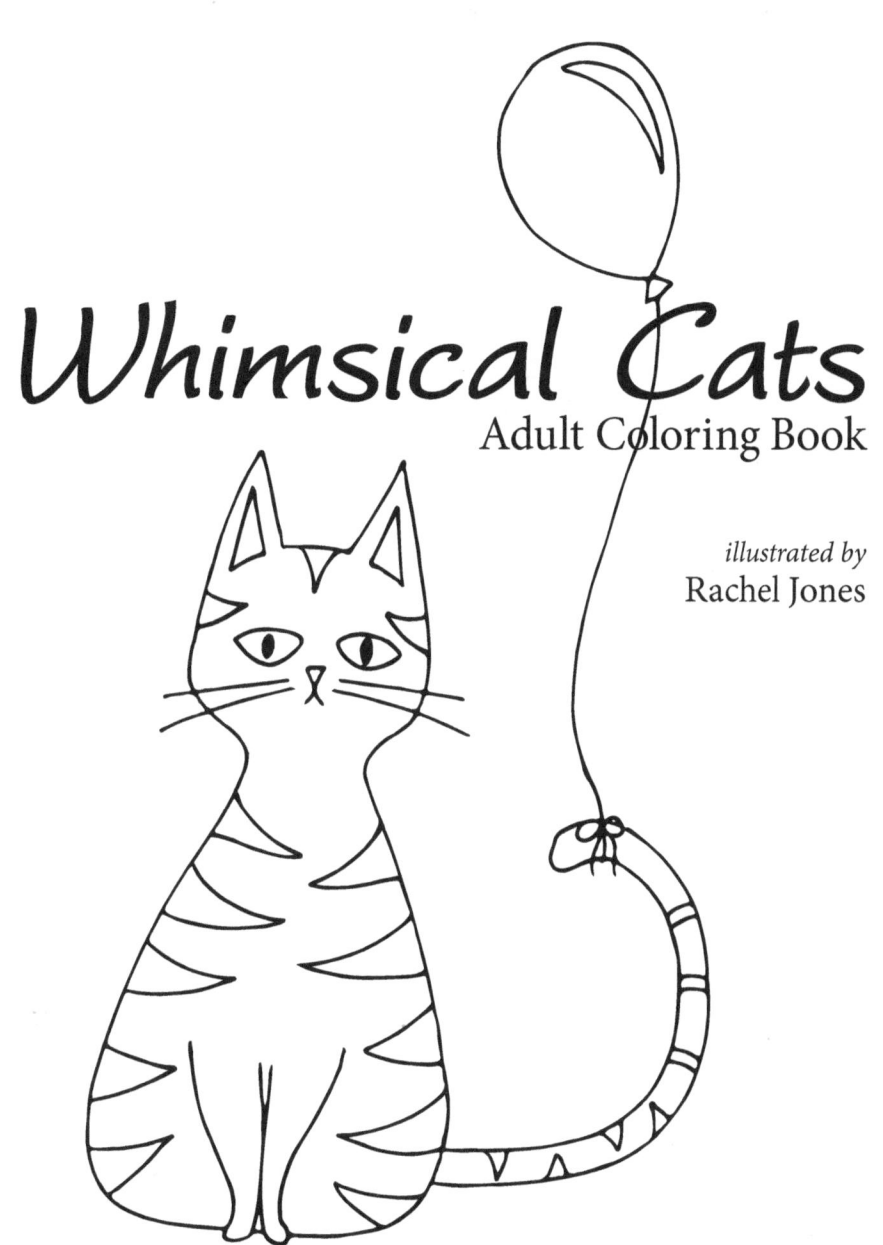

Whimsical Cats
Adult Coloring Book

illustrated by
Rachel Jones

FREE BONUS PAGES
Visit: http://racheljonesarts.com/whimsical-cats/ to receive a PDF of 5 bonus coloring pages.

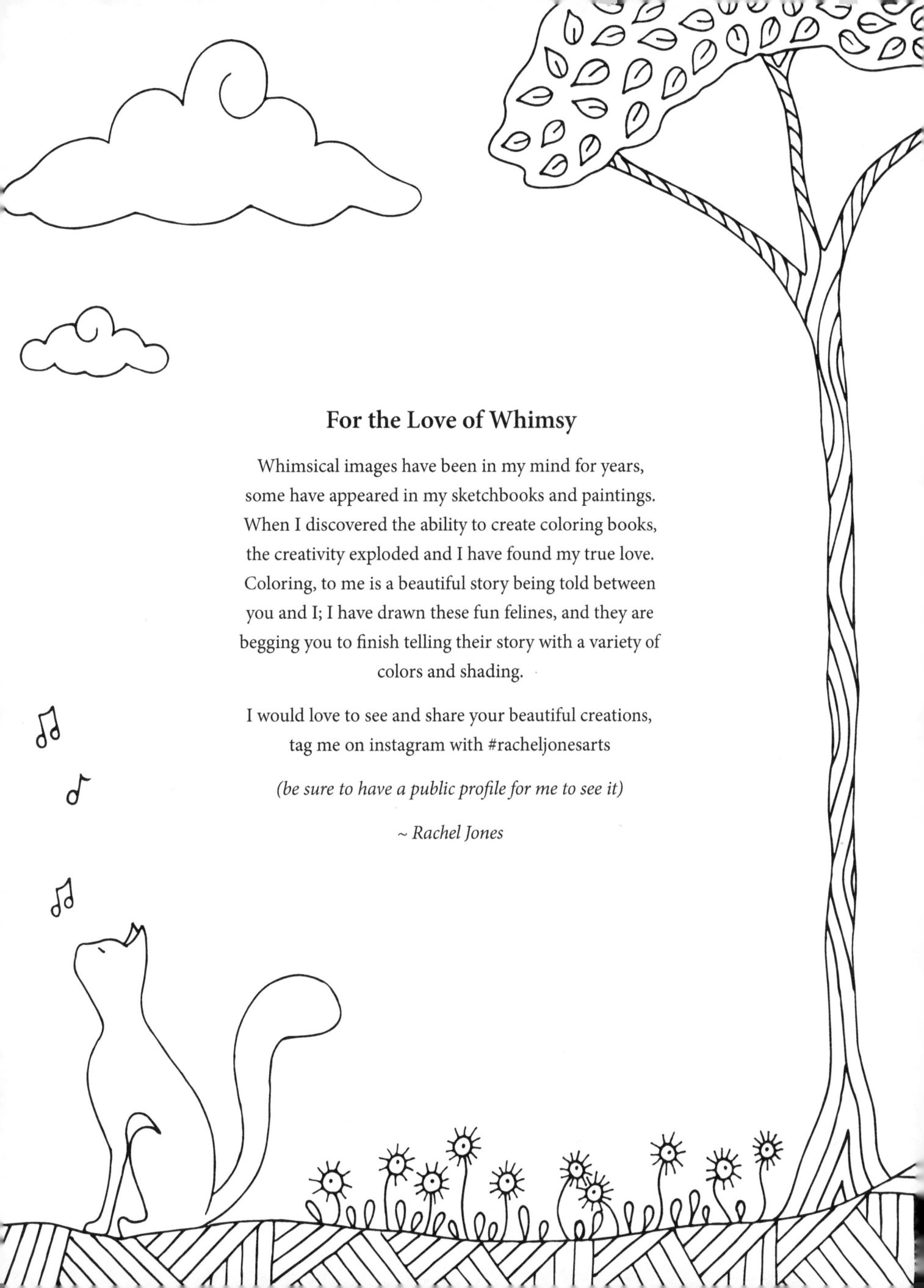

For the Love of Whimsy

Whimsical images have been in my mind for years,
some have appeared in my sketchbooks and paintings.
When I discovered the ability to create coloring books,
the creativity exploded and I have found my true love.
Coloring, to me is a beautiful story being told between
you and I; I have drawn these fun felines, and they are
begging you to finish telling their story with a variety of
colors and shading.

I would love to see and share your beautiful creations,
tag me on instagram with #racheljonesarts

(be sure to have a public profile for me to see it)

~ Rachel Jones

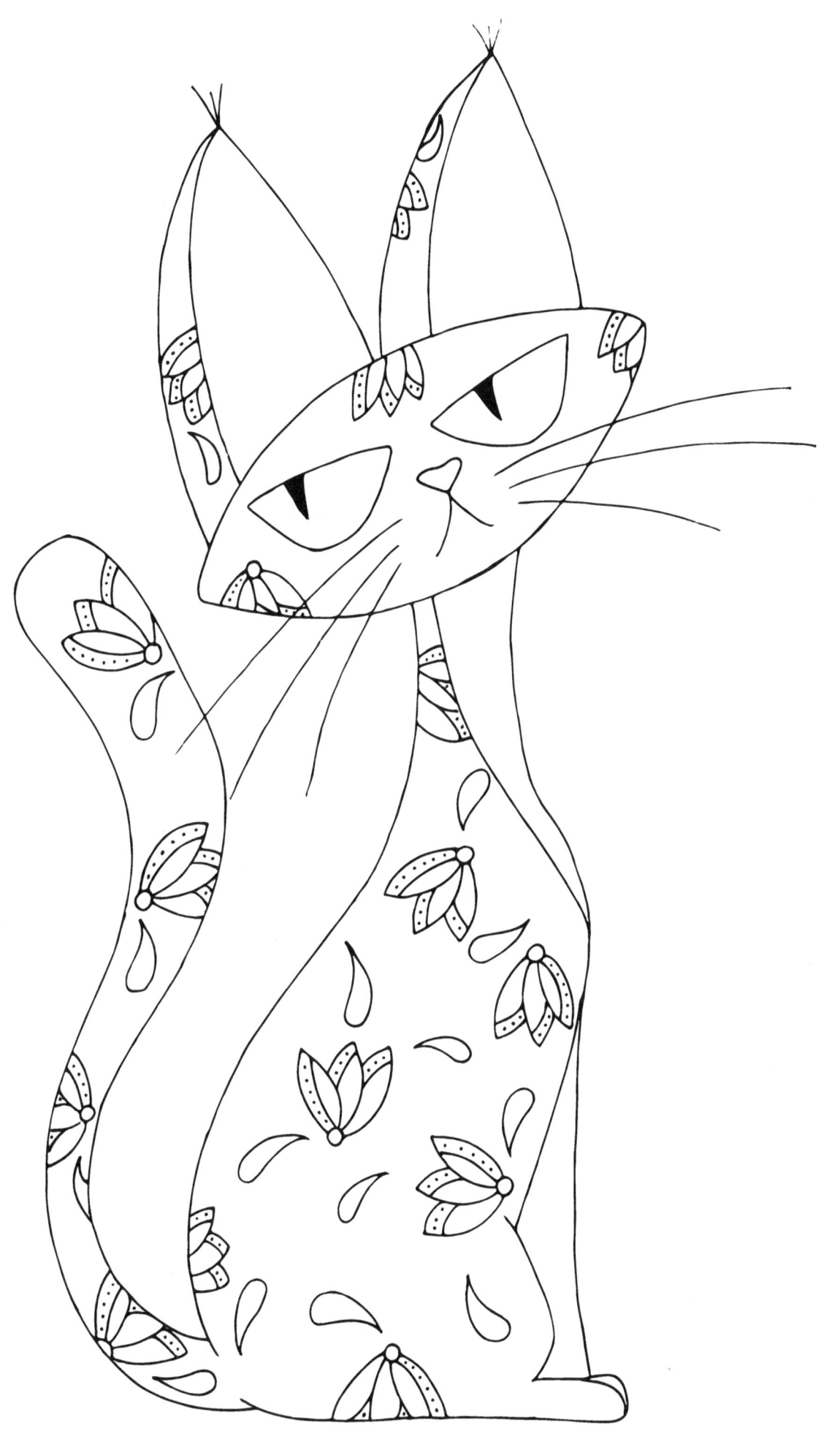

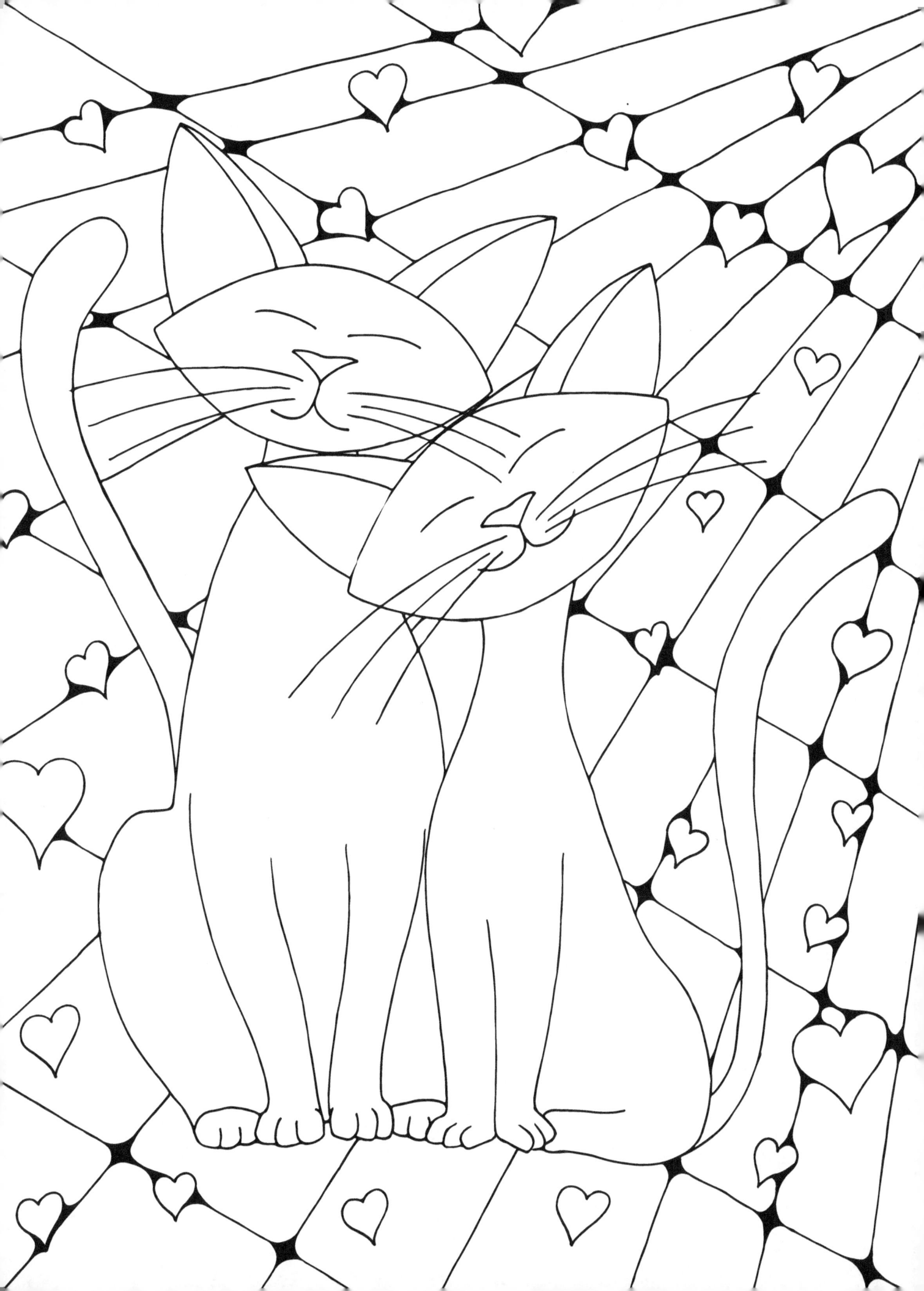

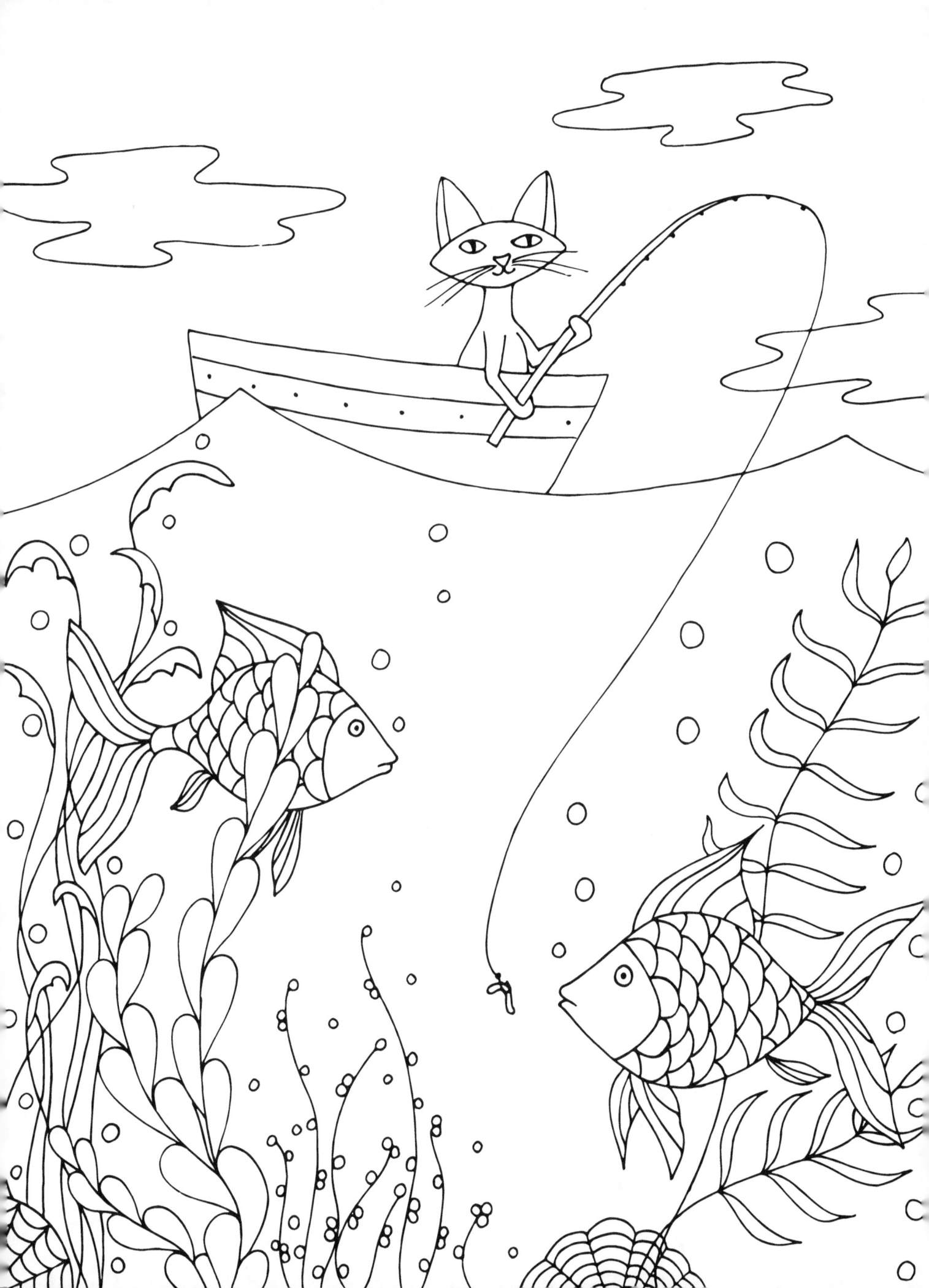

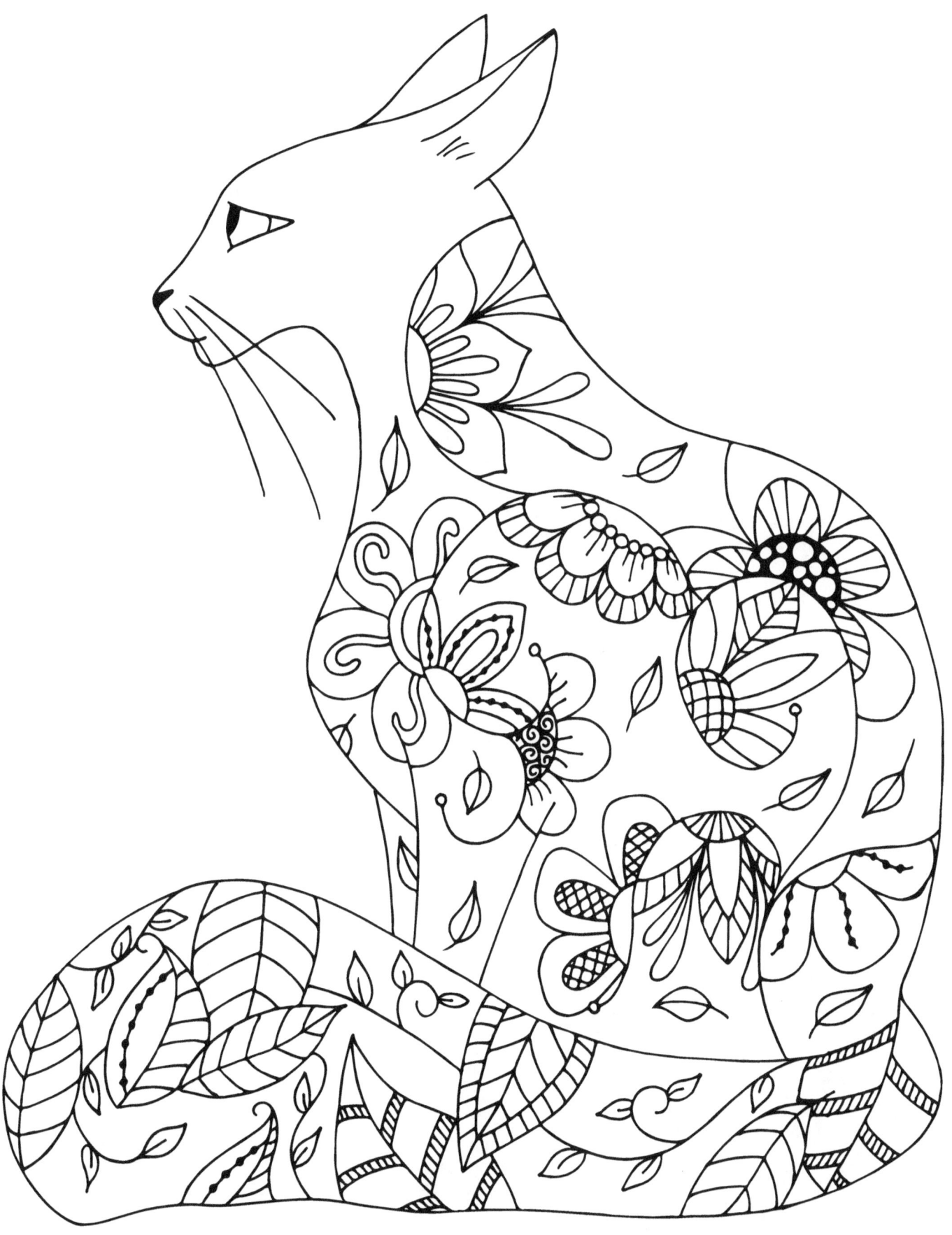

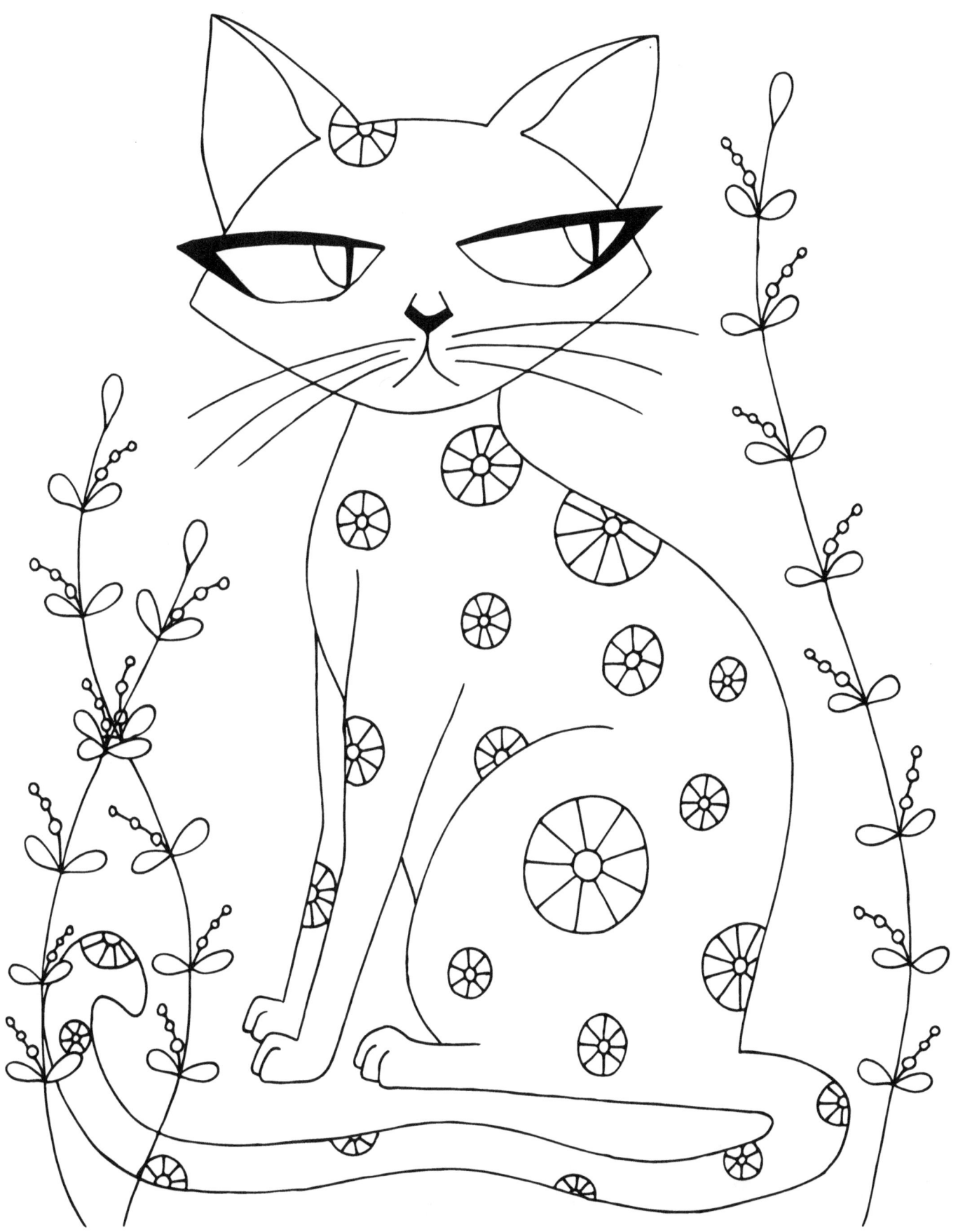

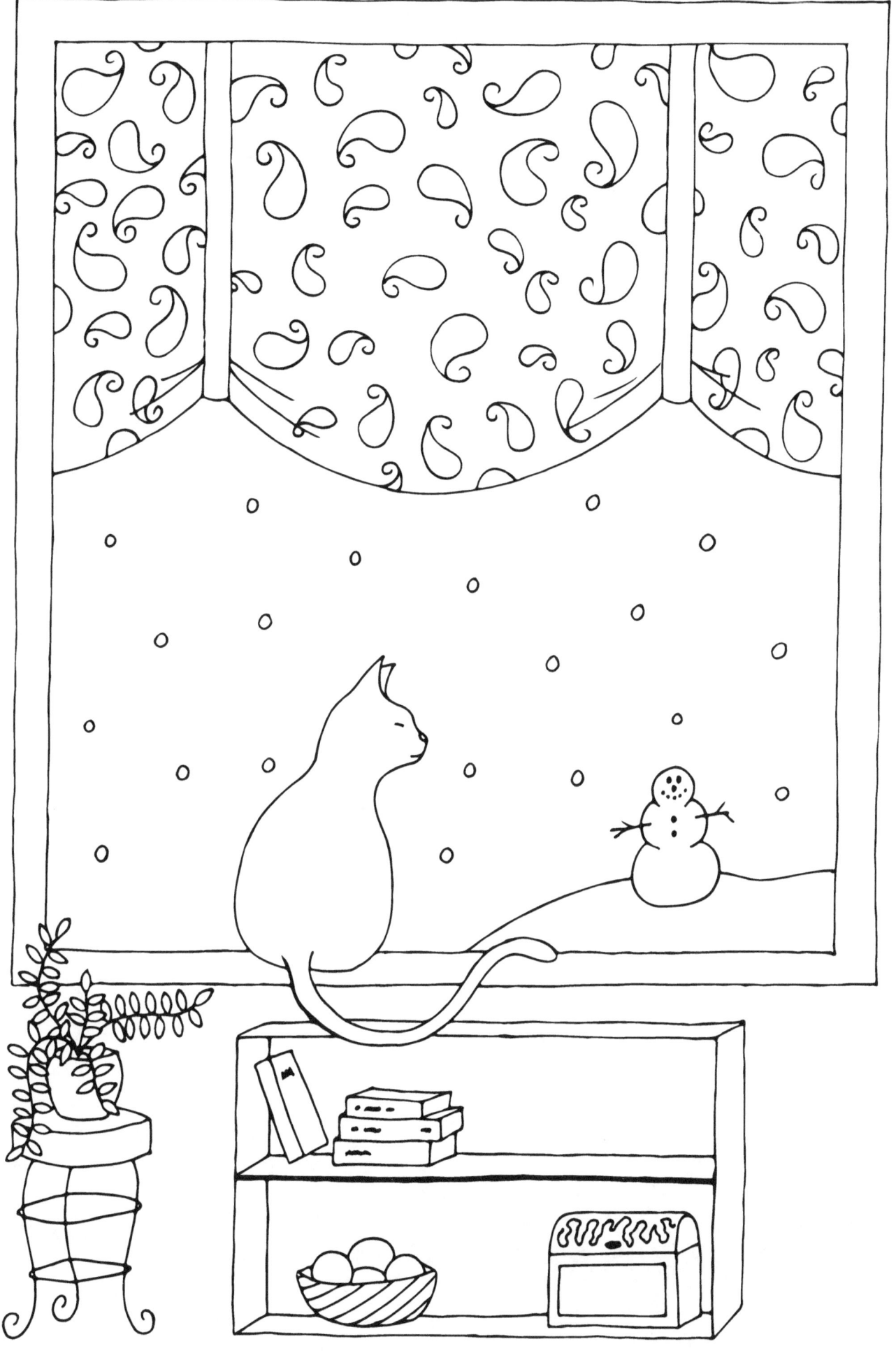

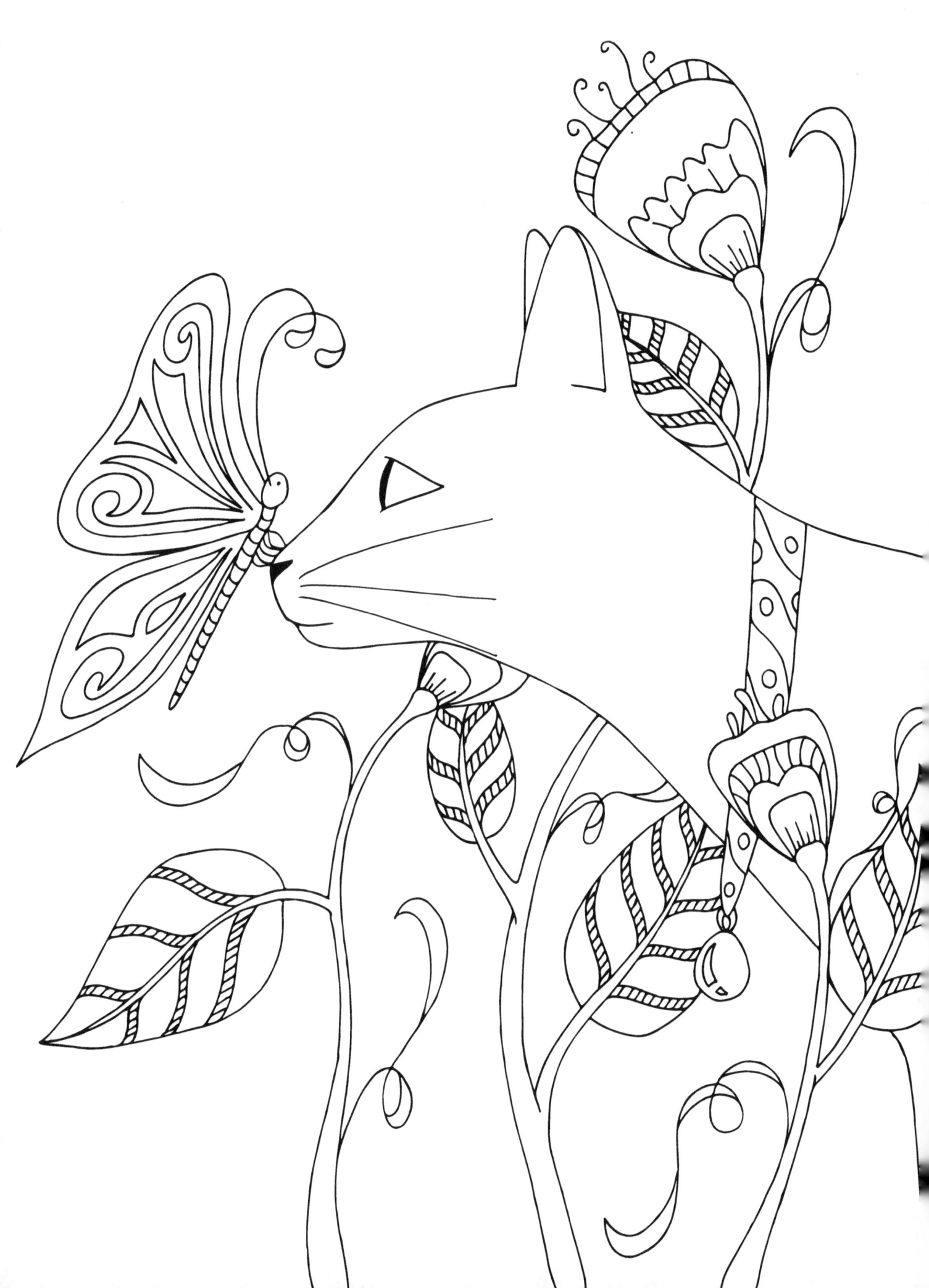

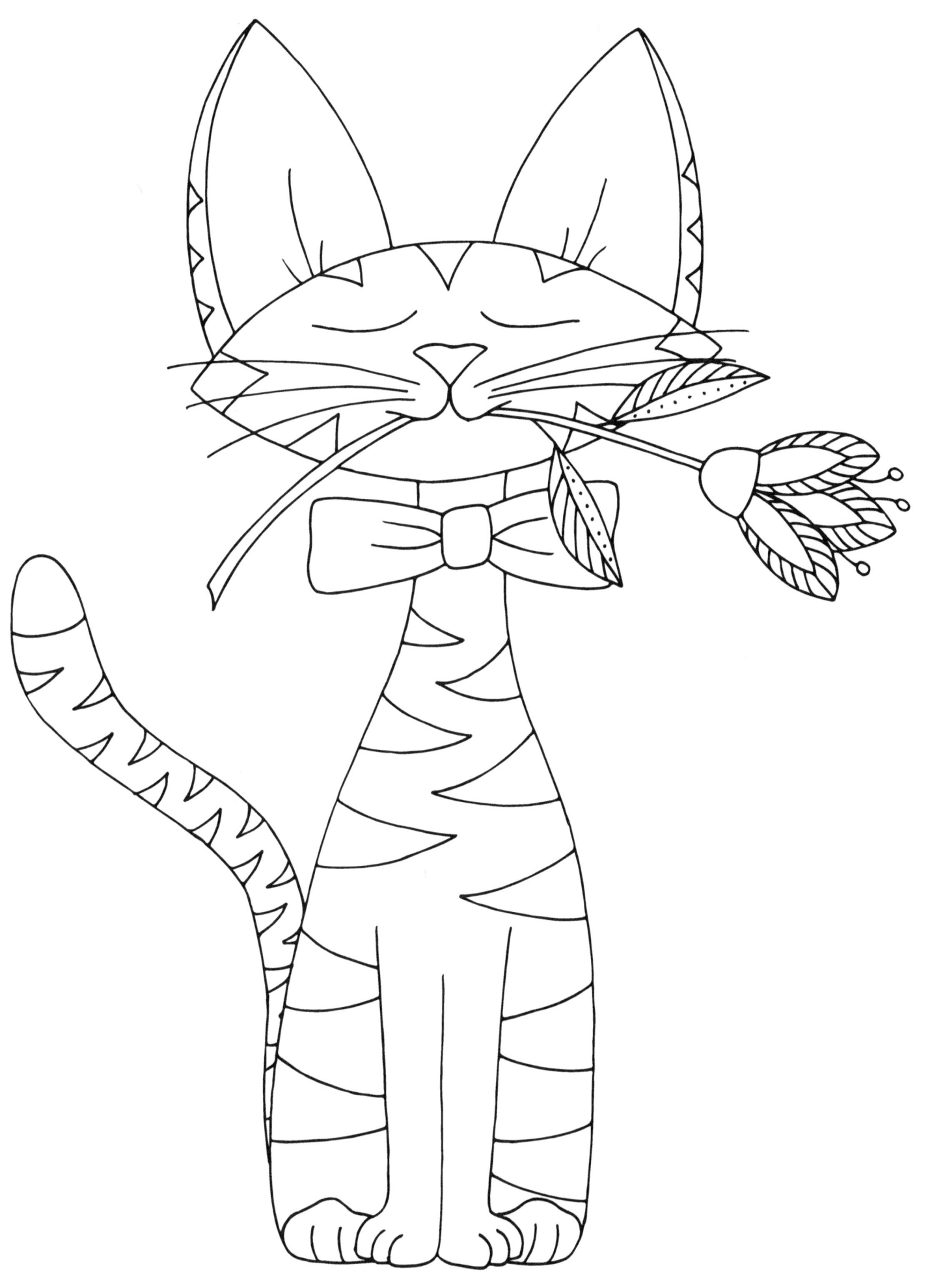

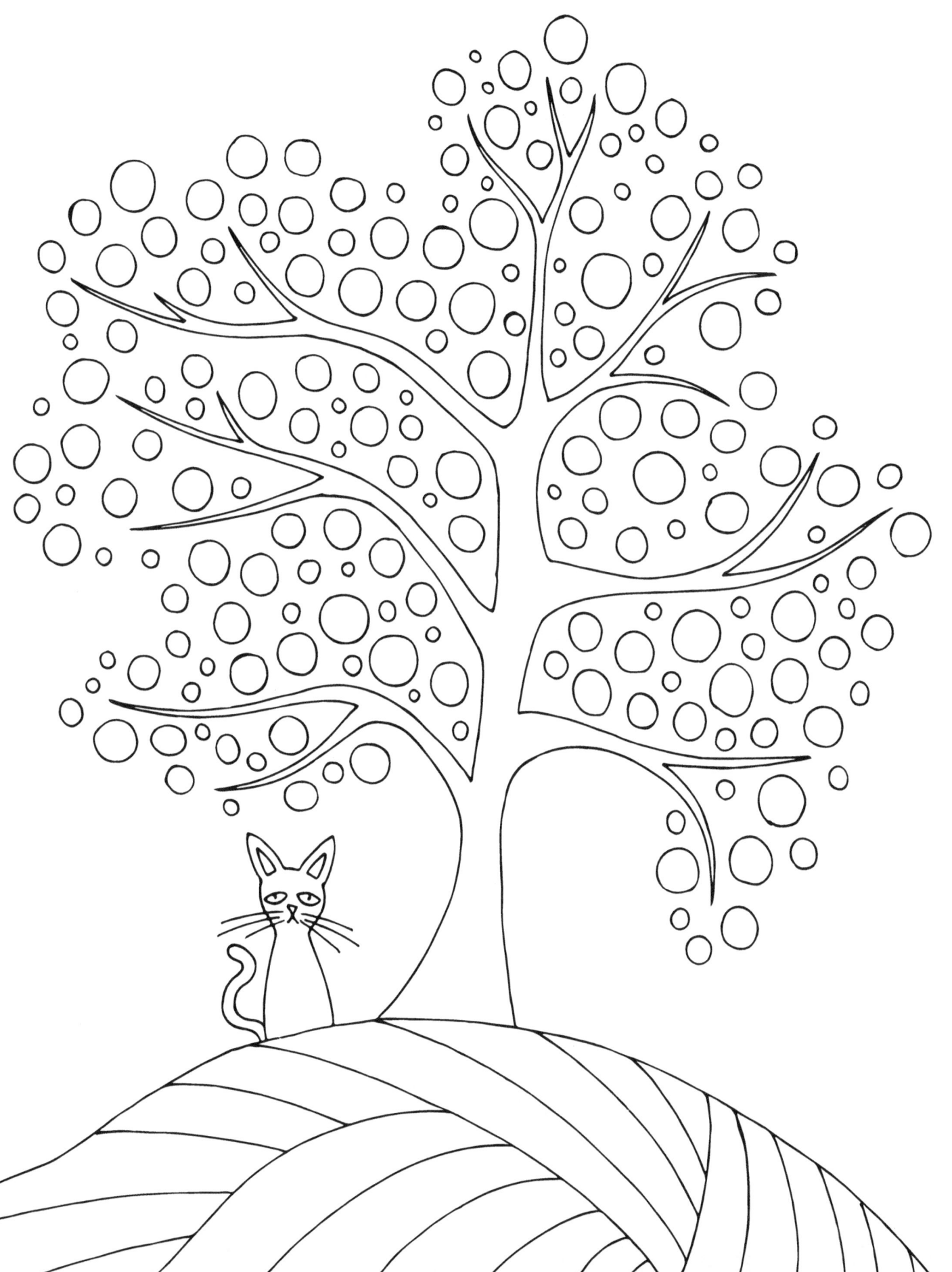

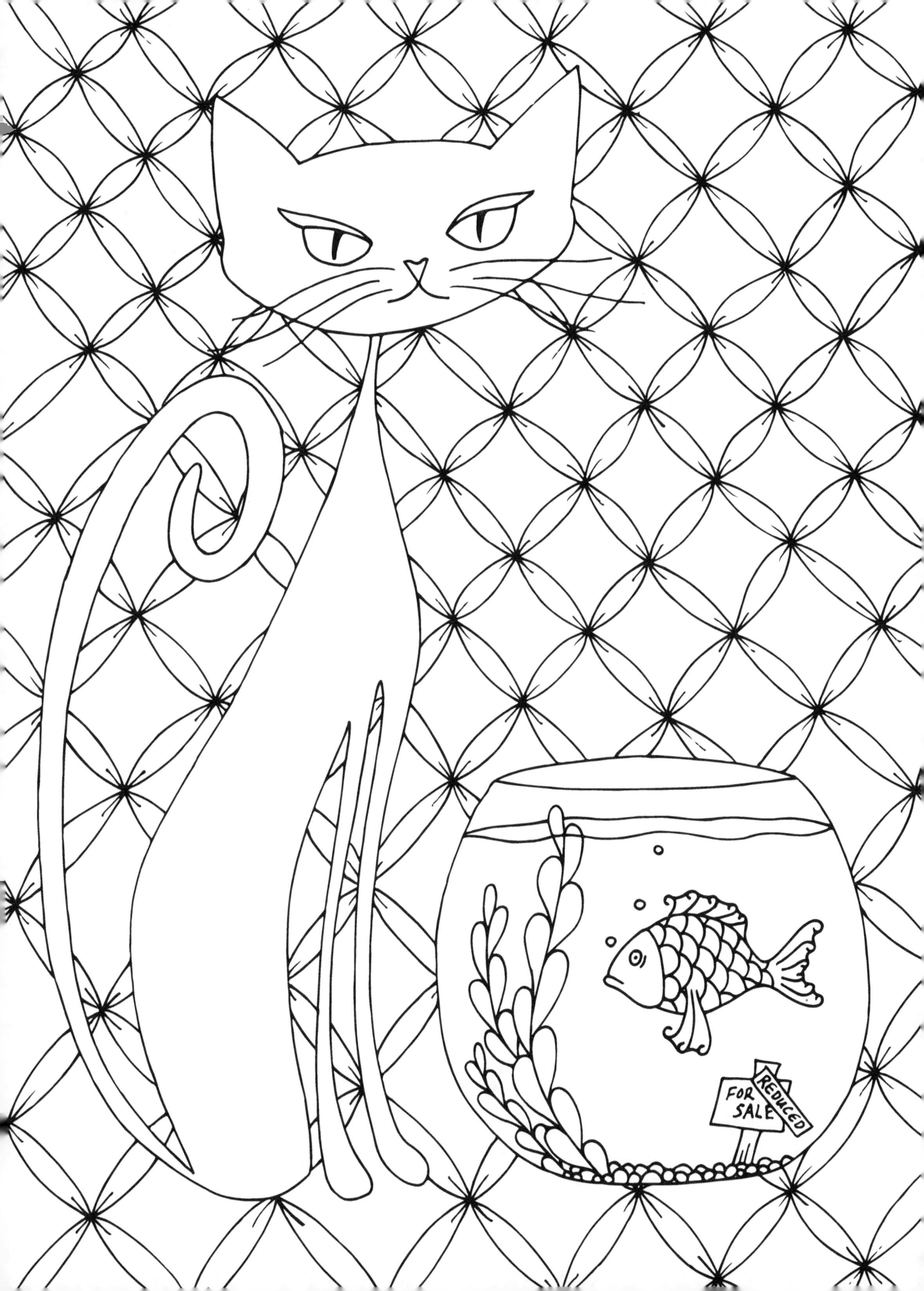

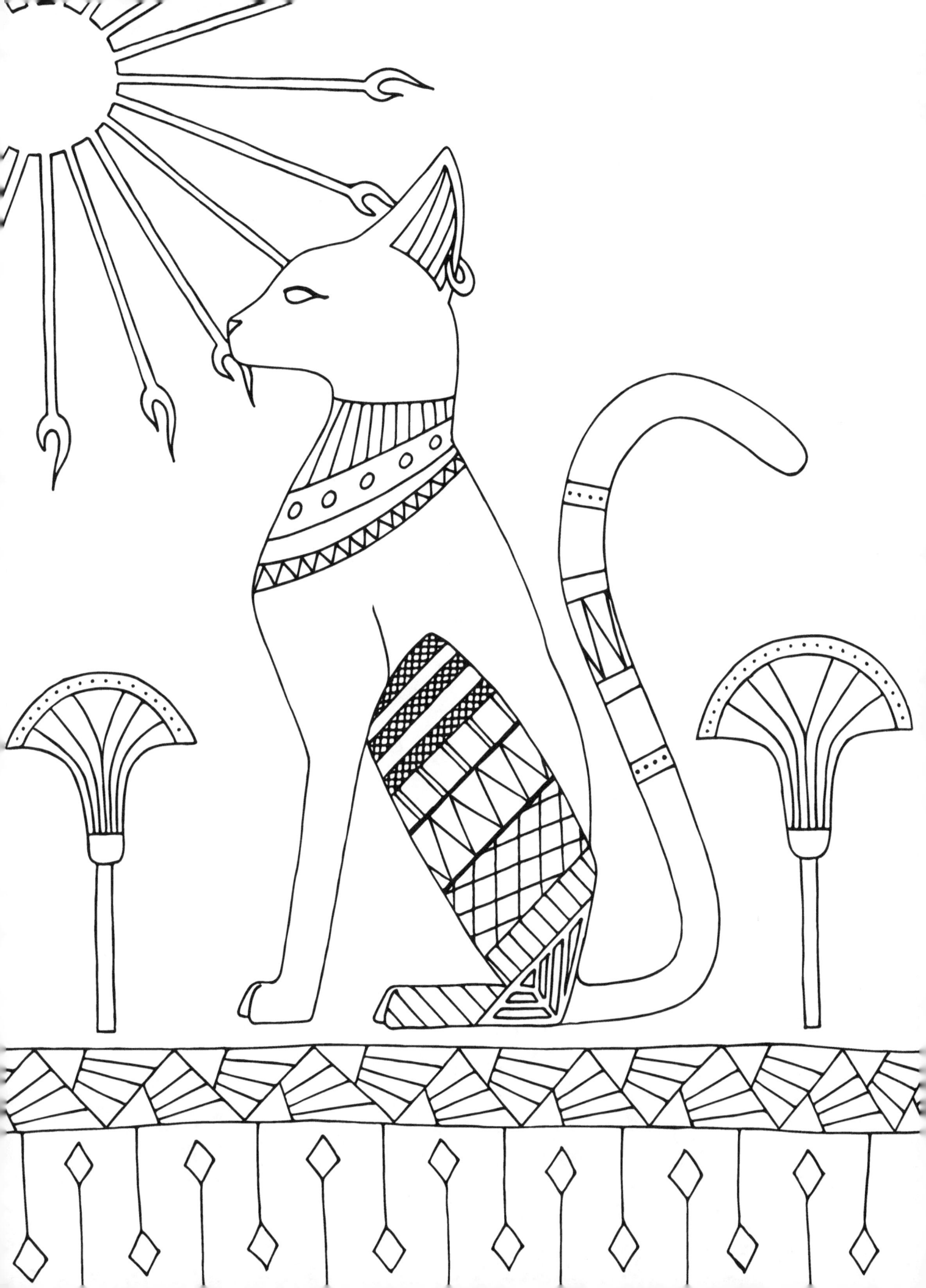

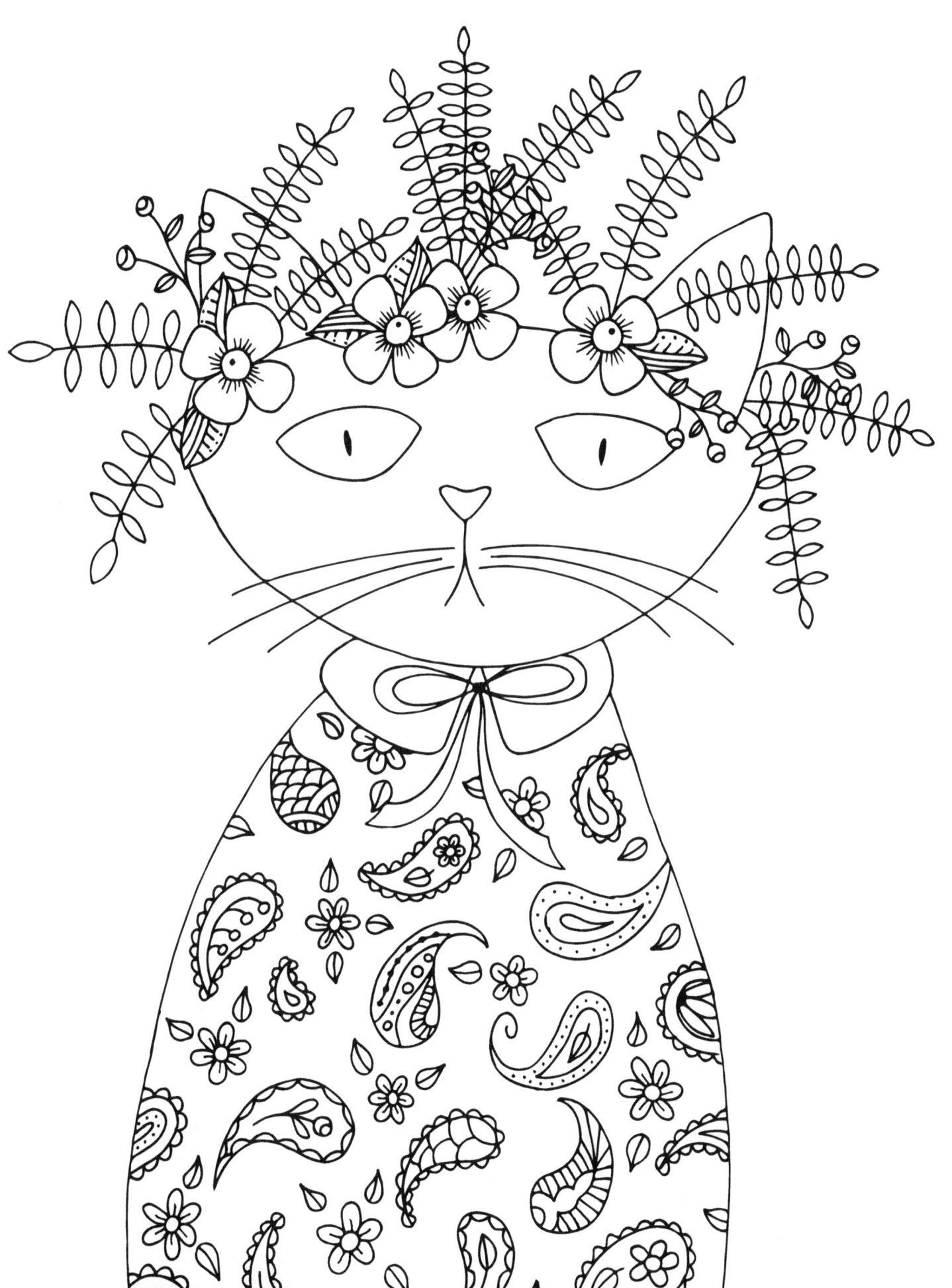

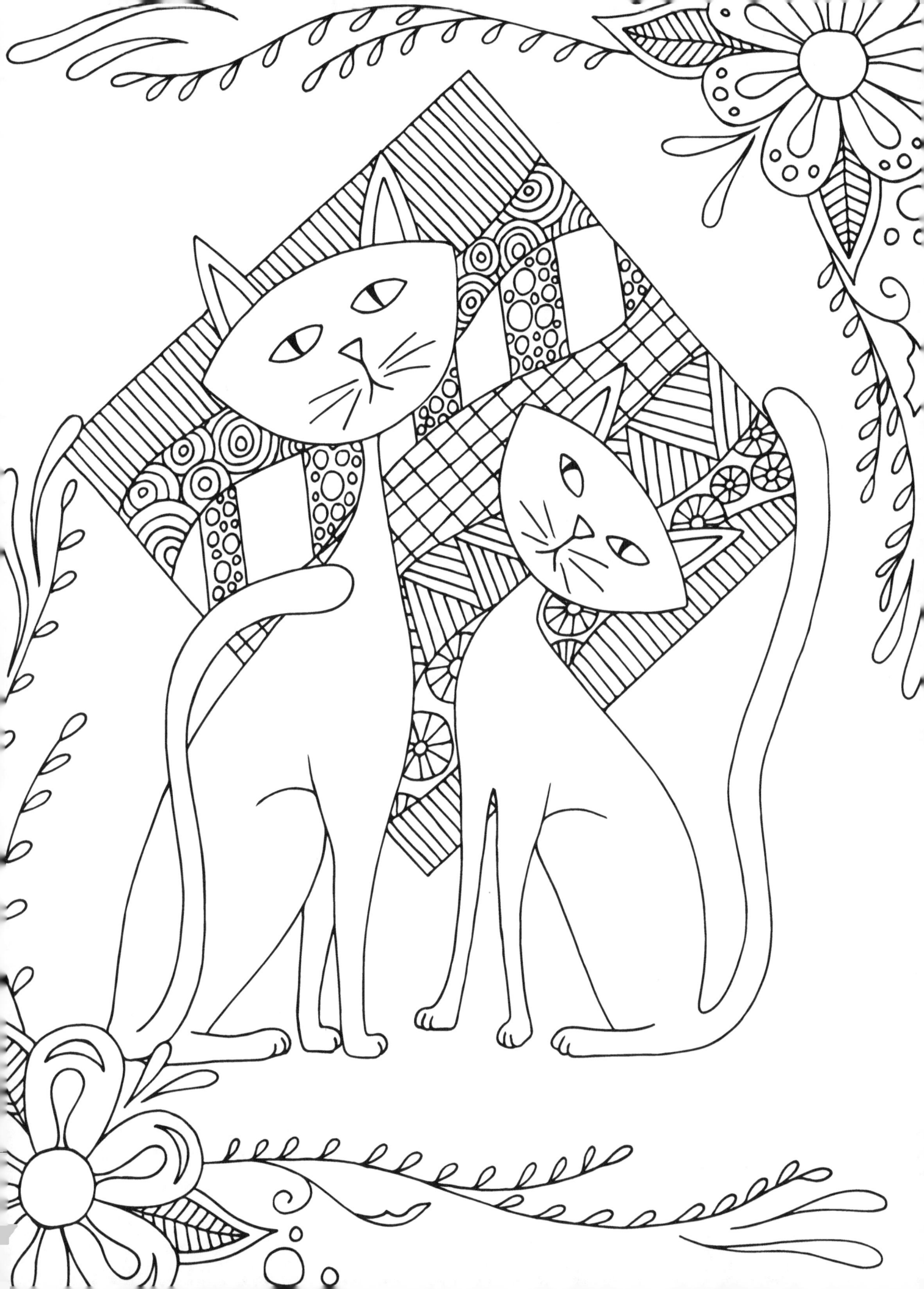

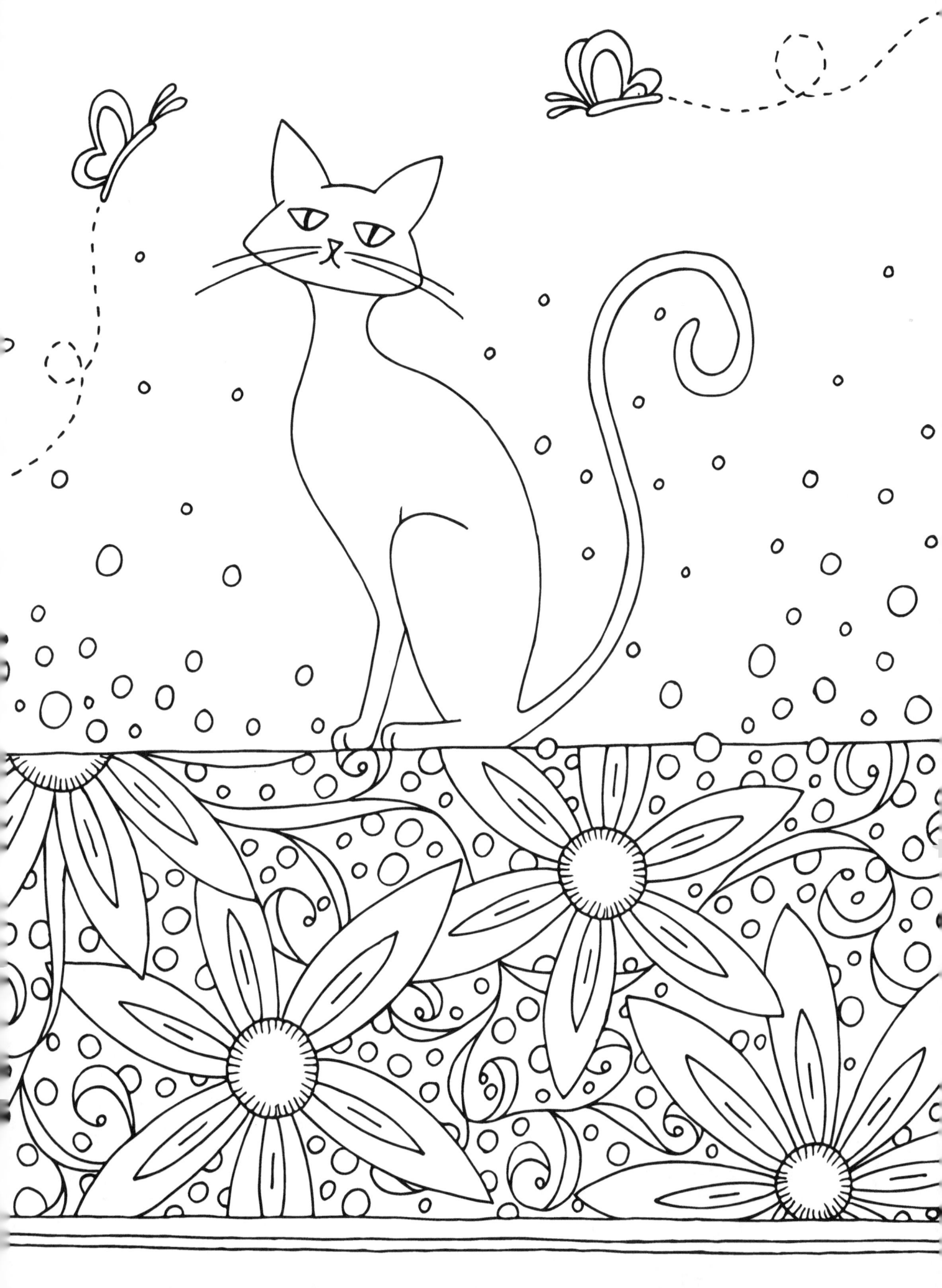

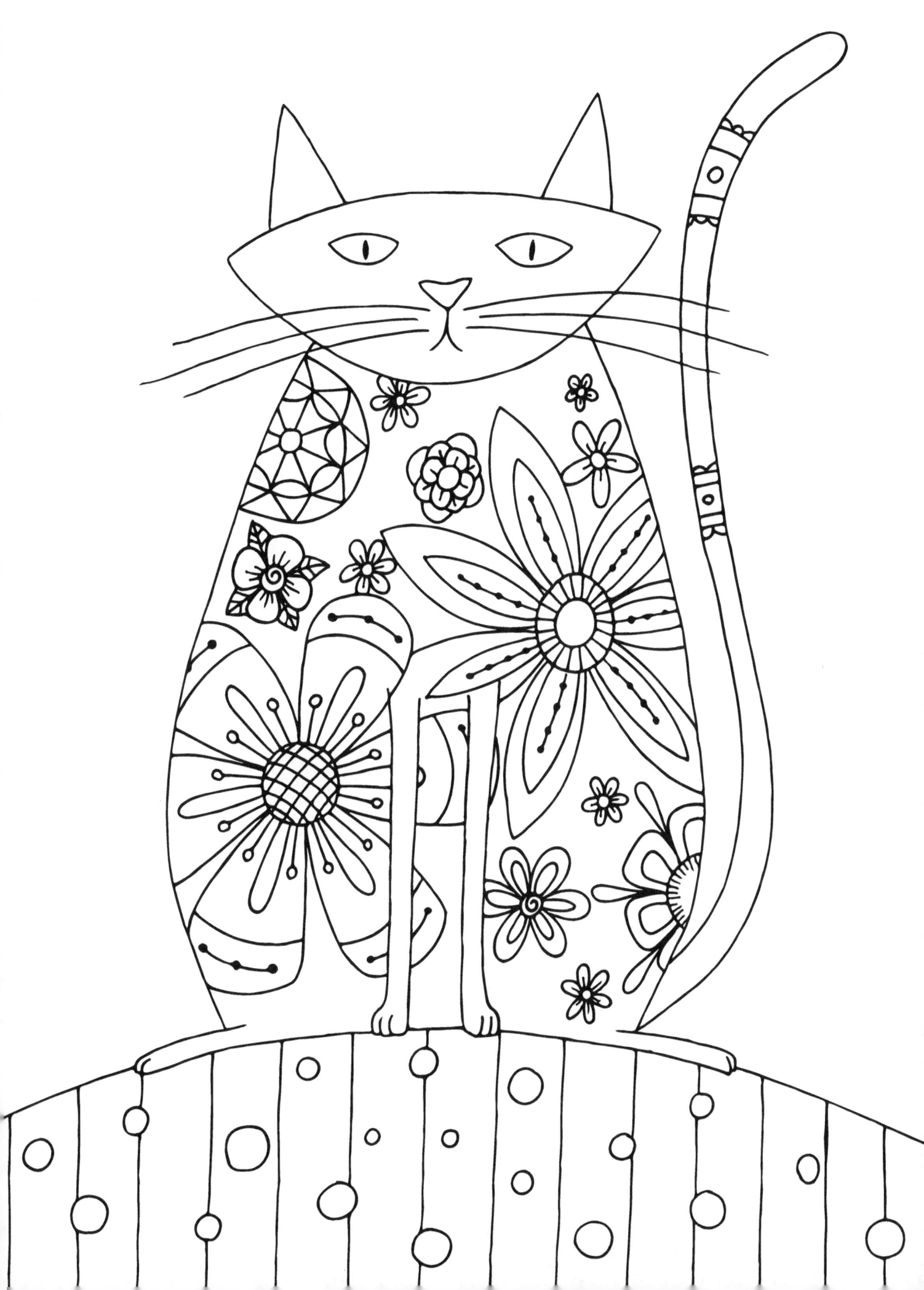

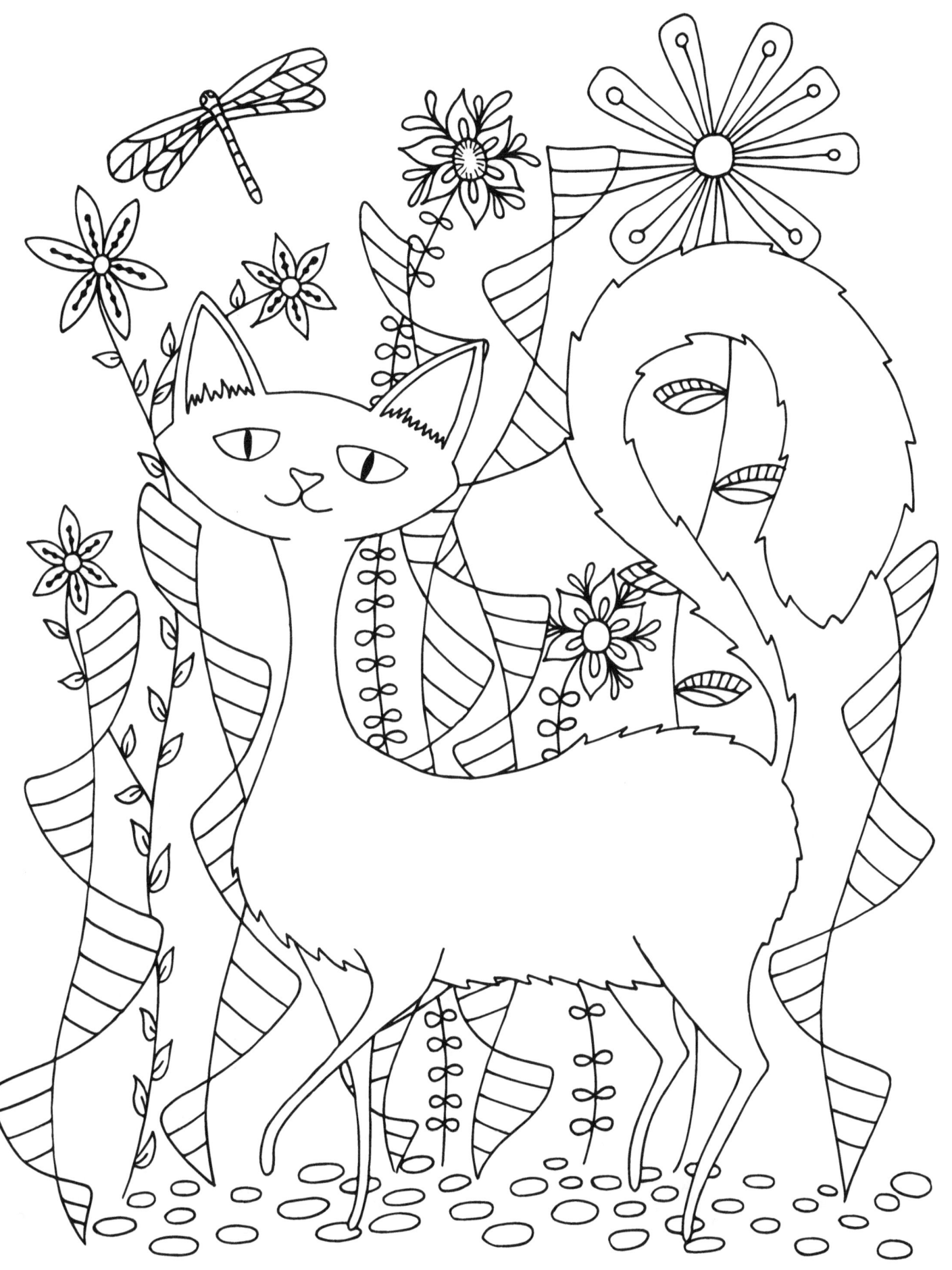

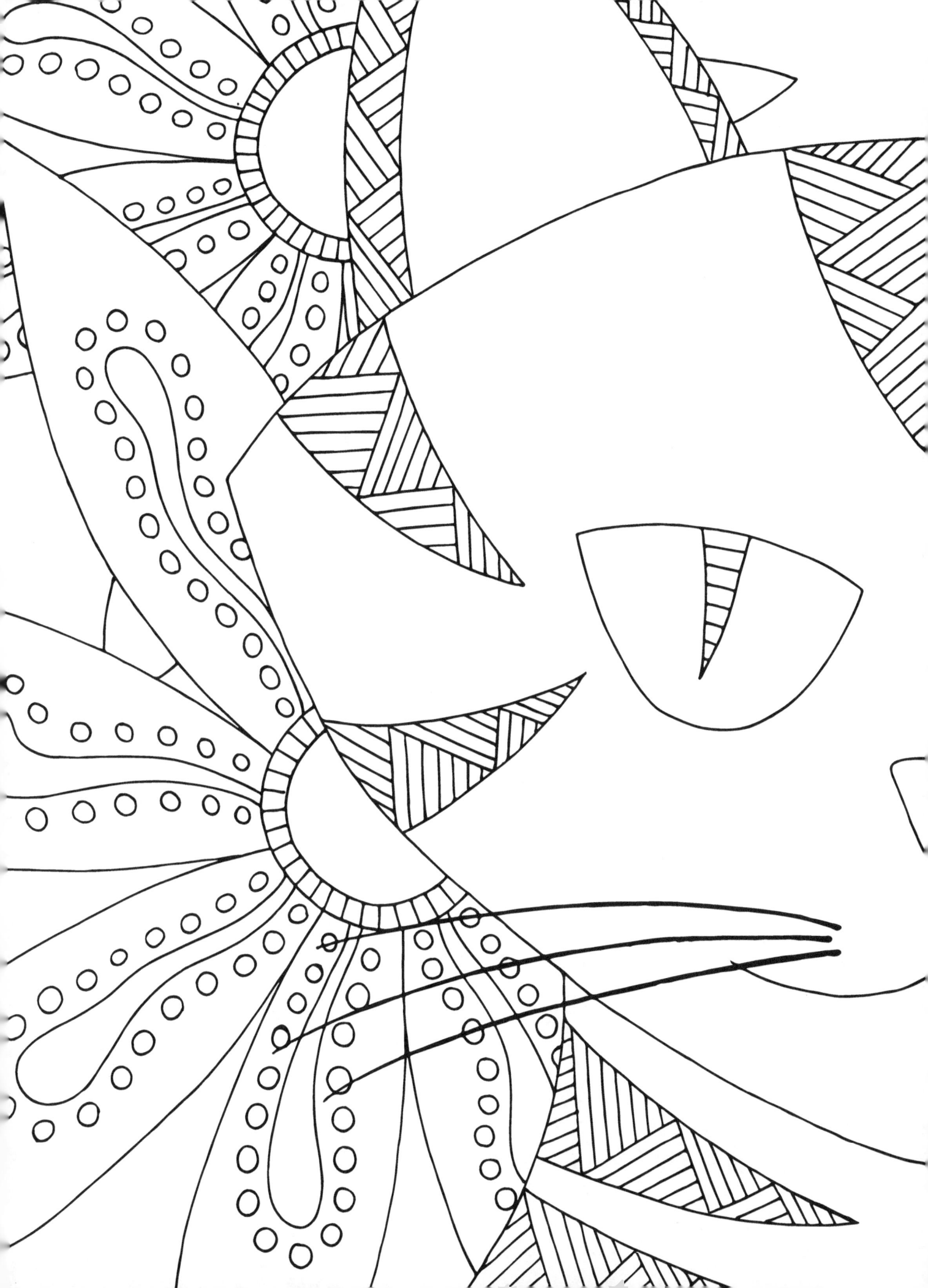

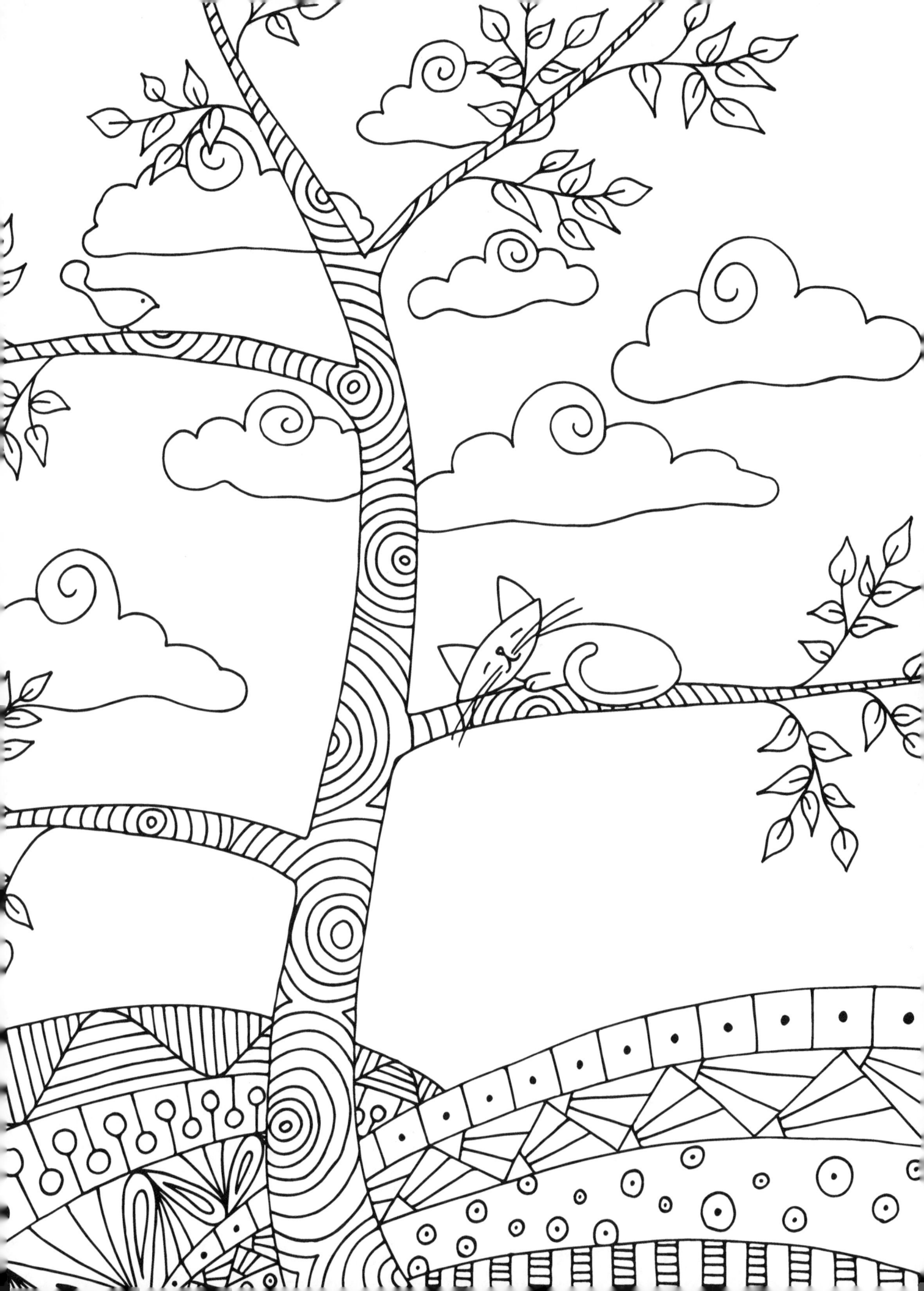

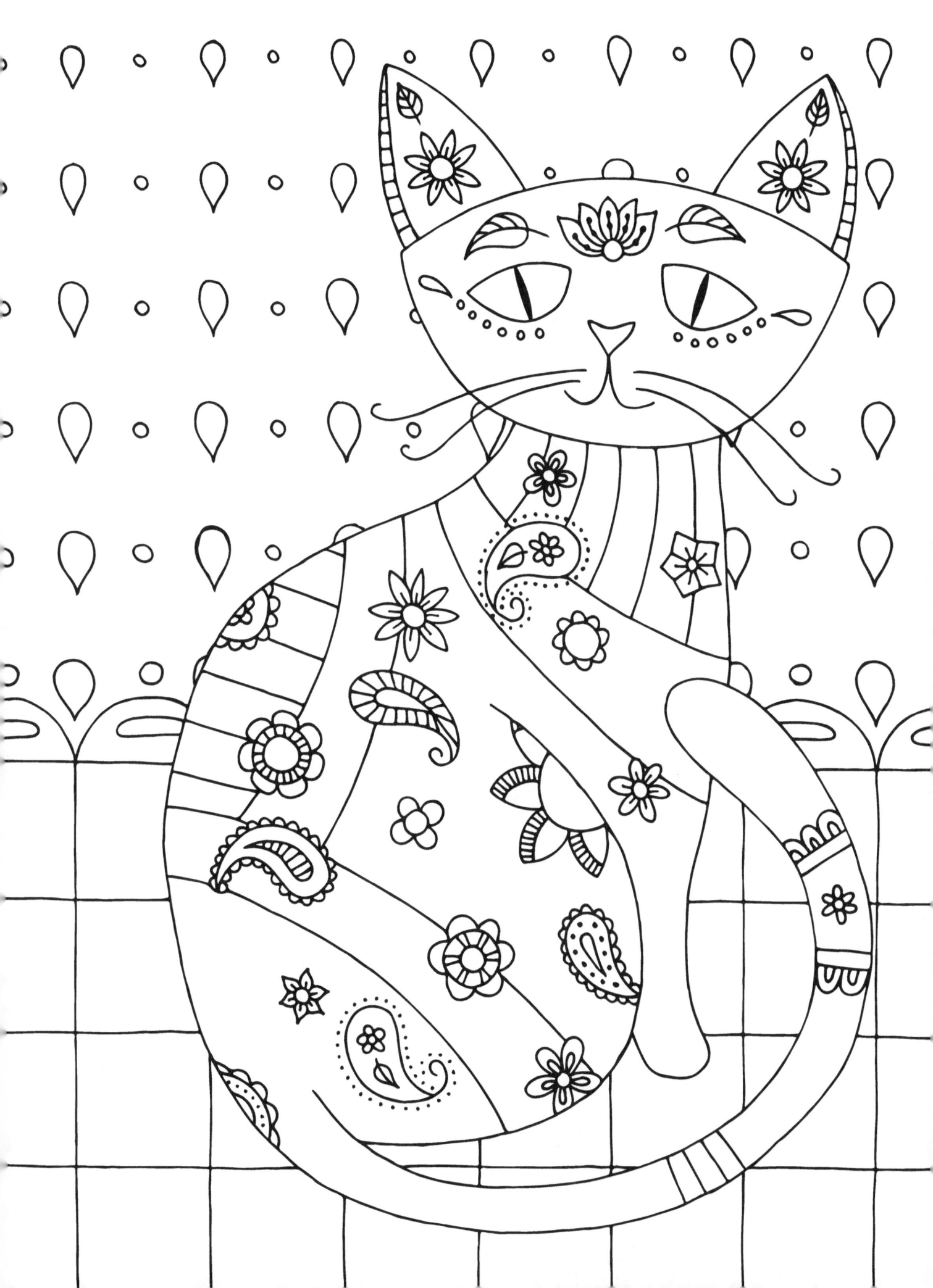

What greater gift Than the Love of a Cat

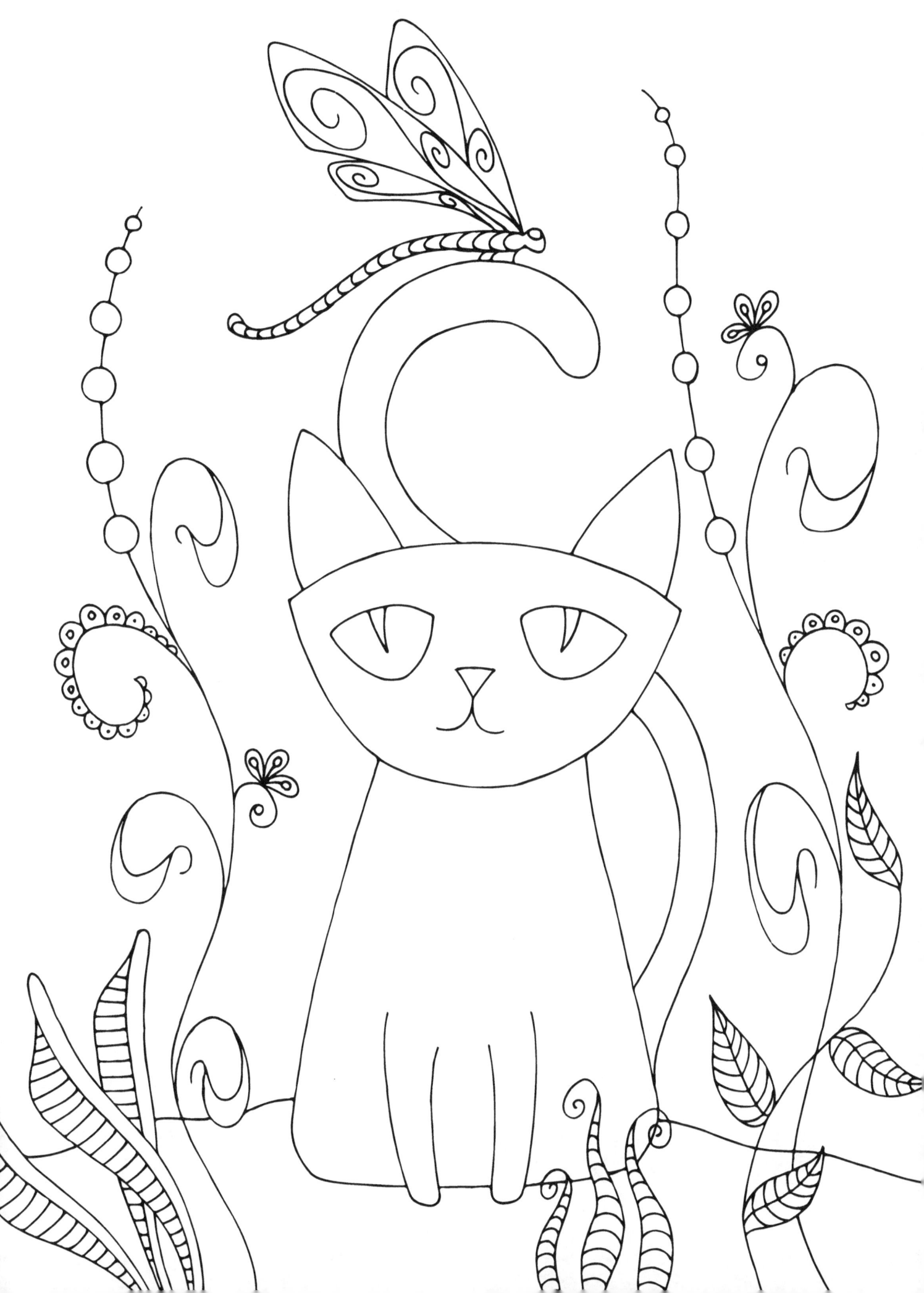

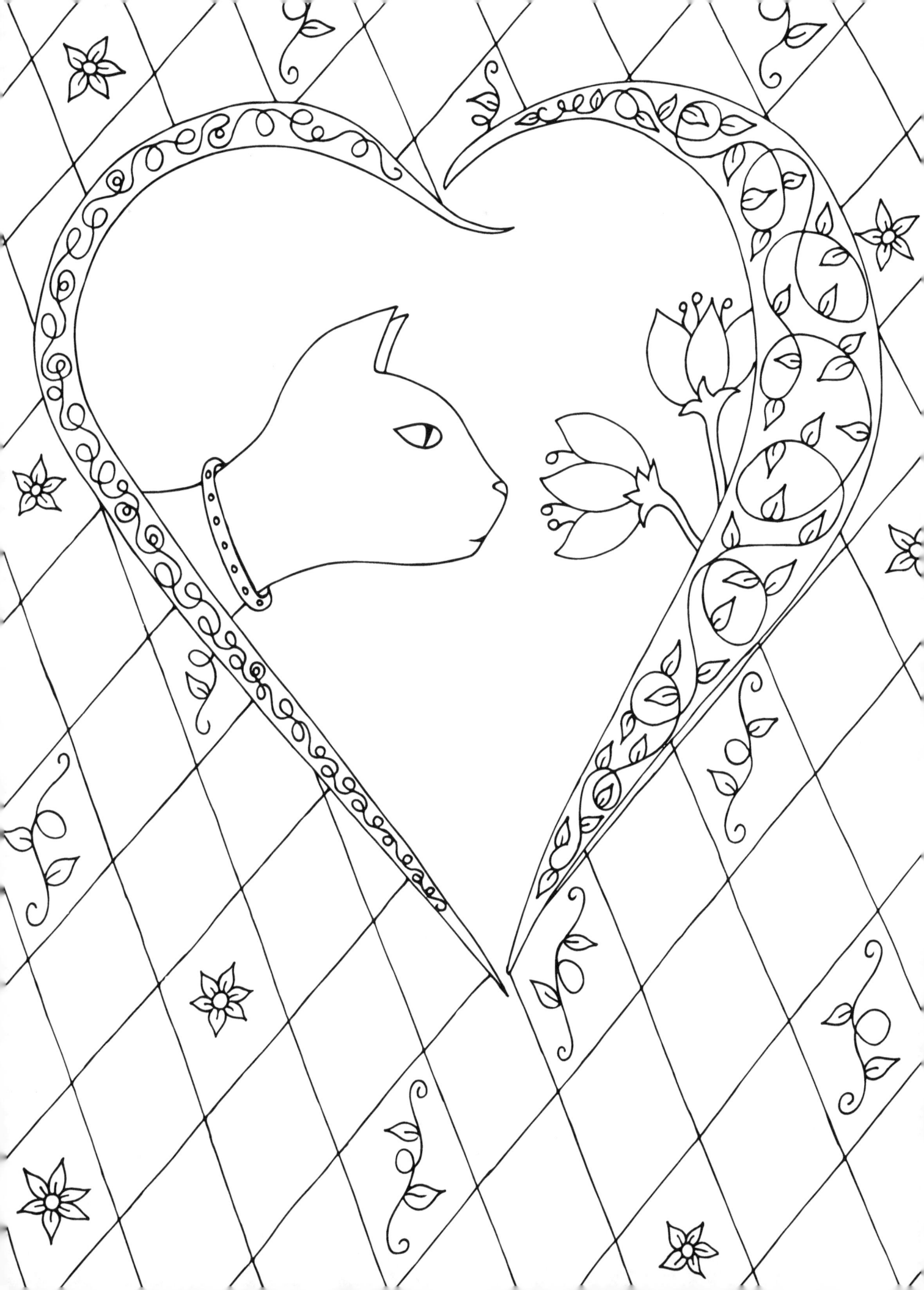

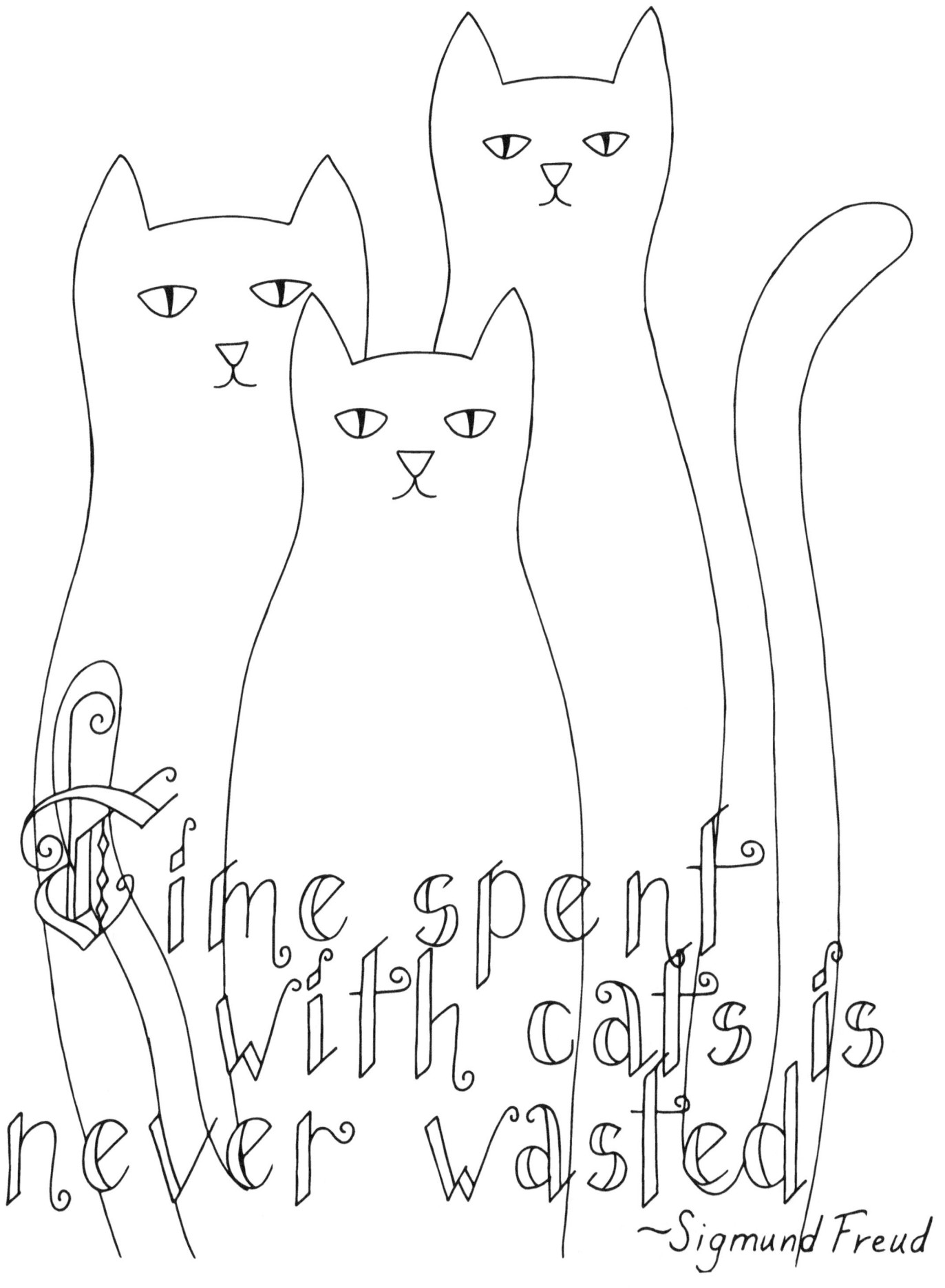

Time spent with cats is never wasted

~Sigmund Freud

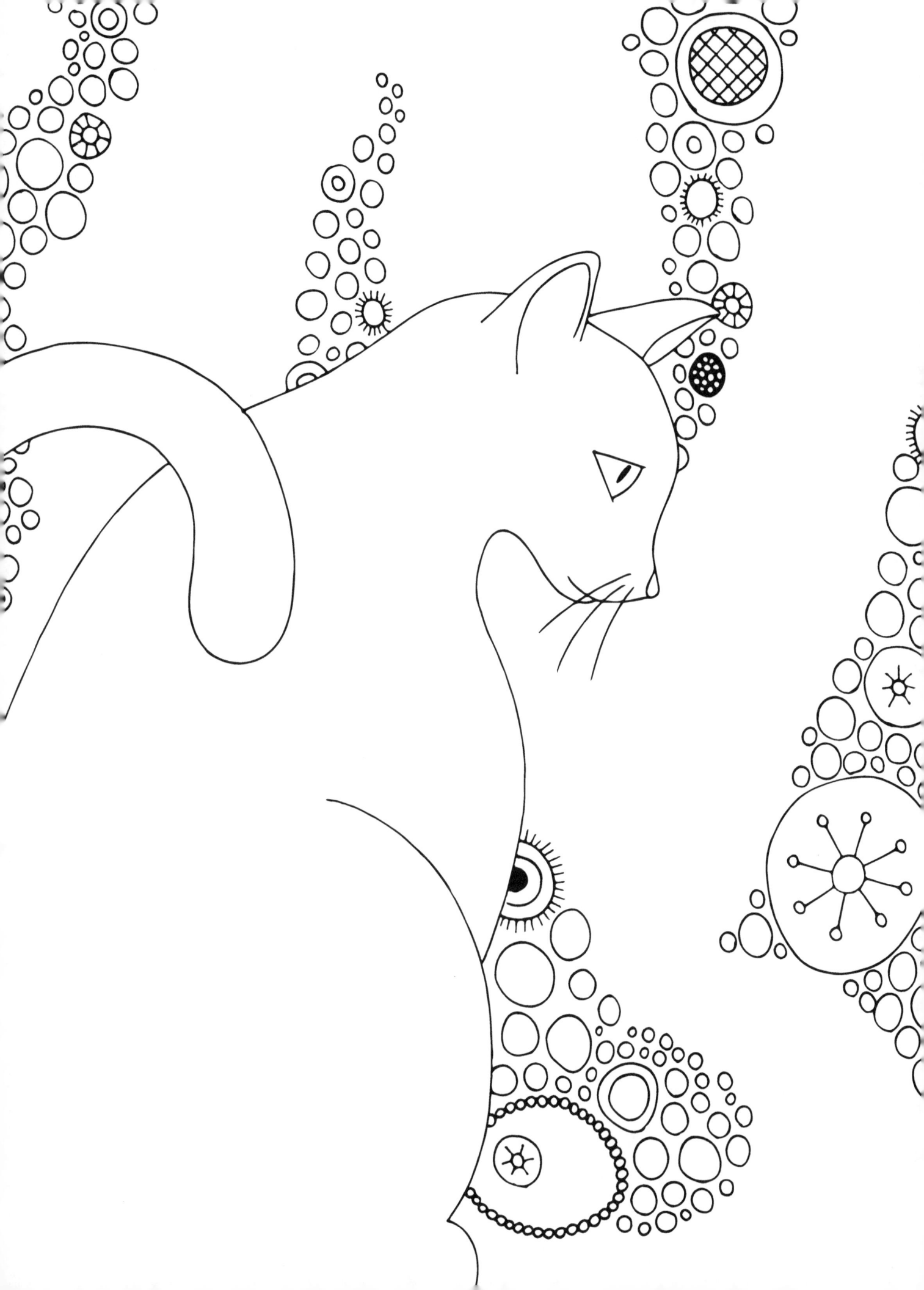

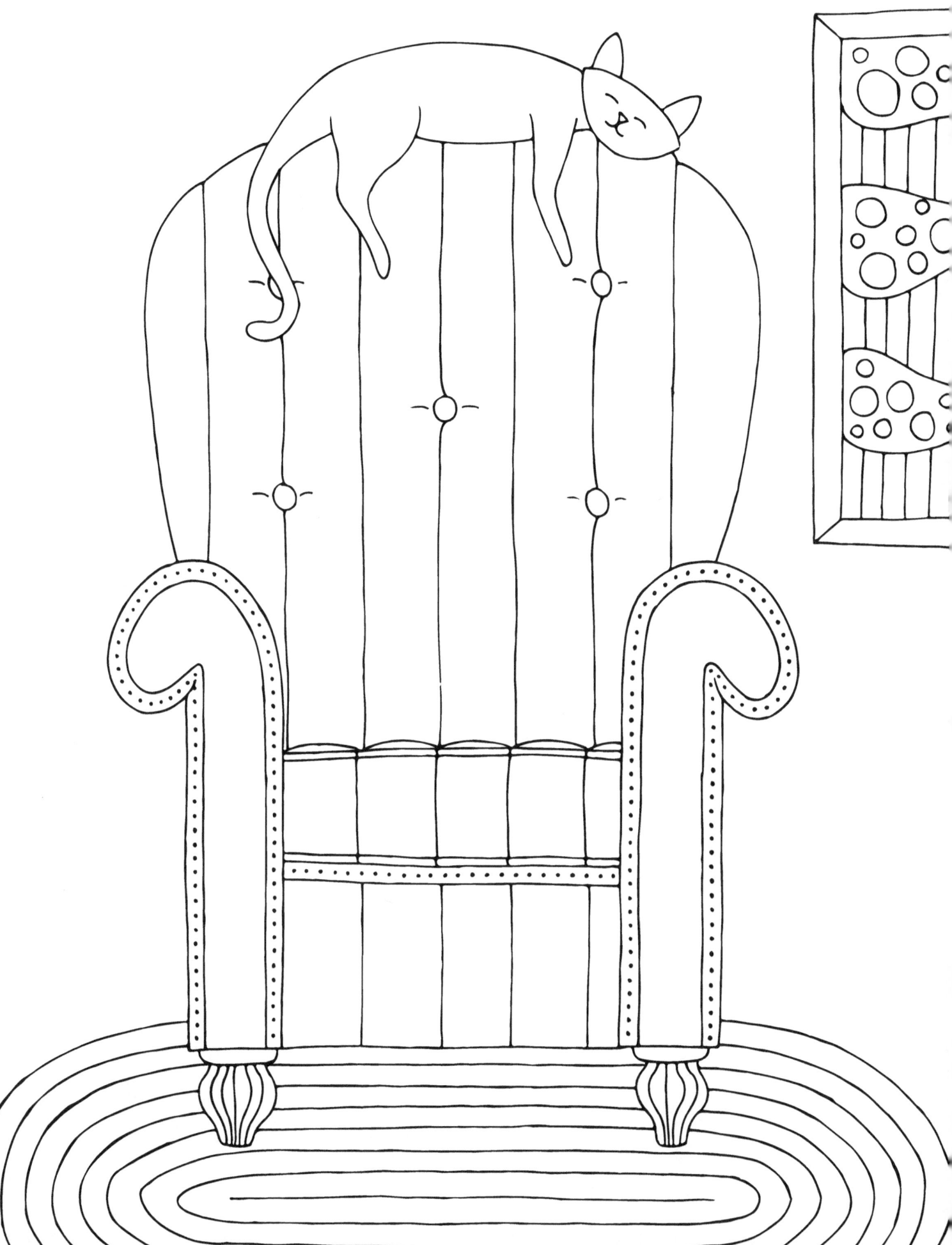

Home is
where the
Cat is

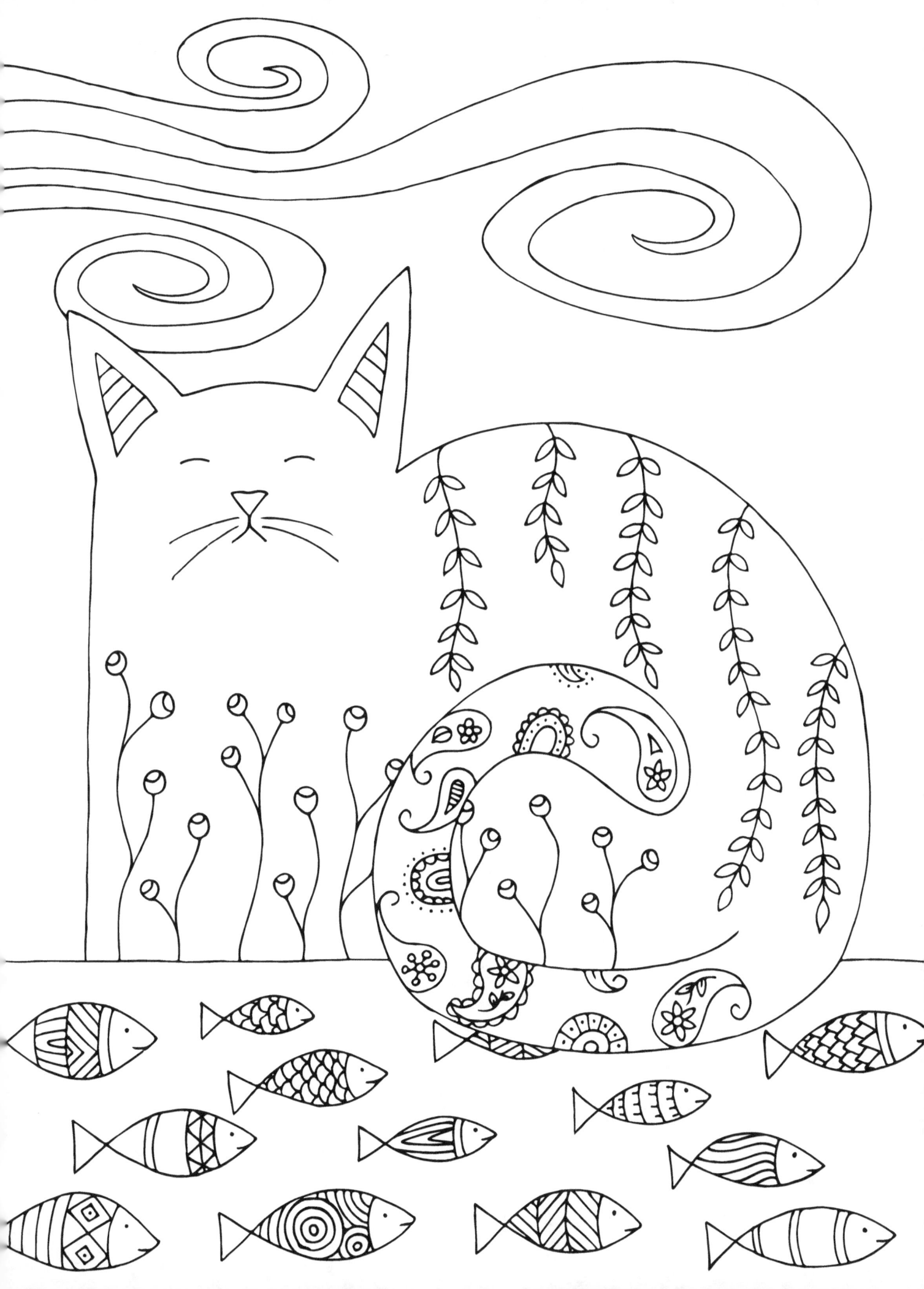

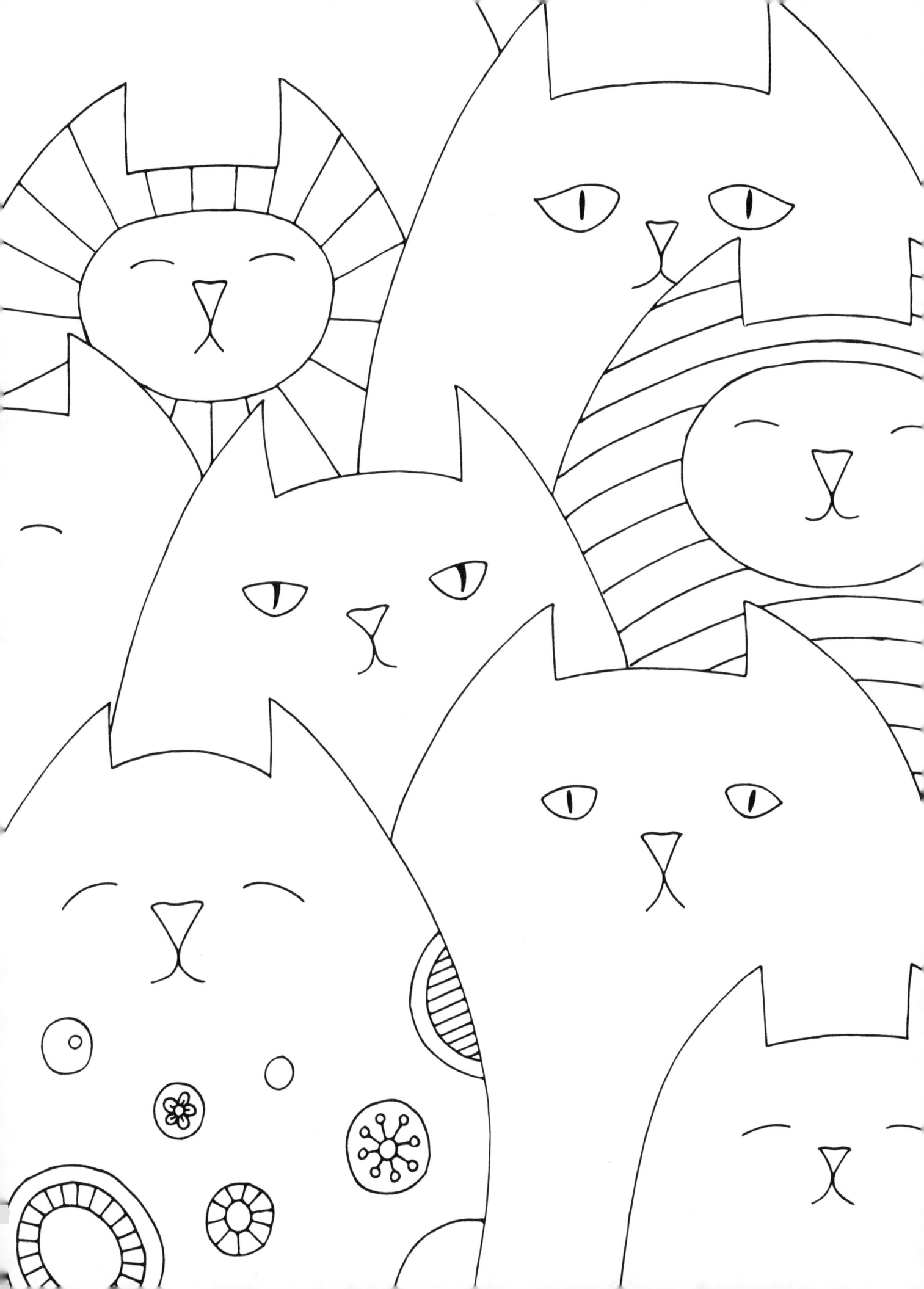

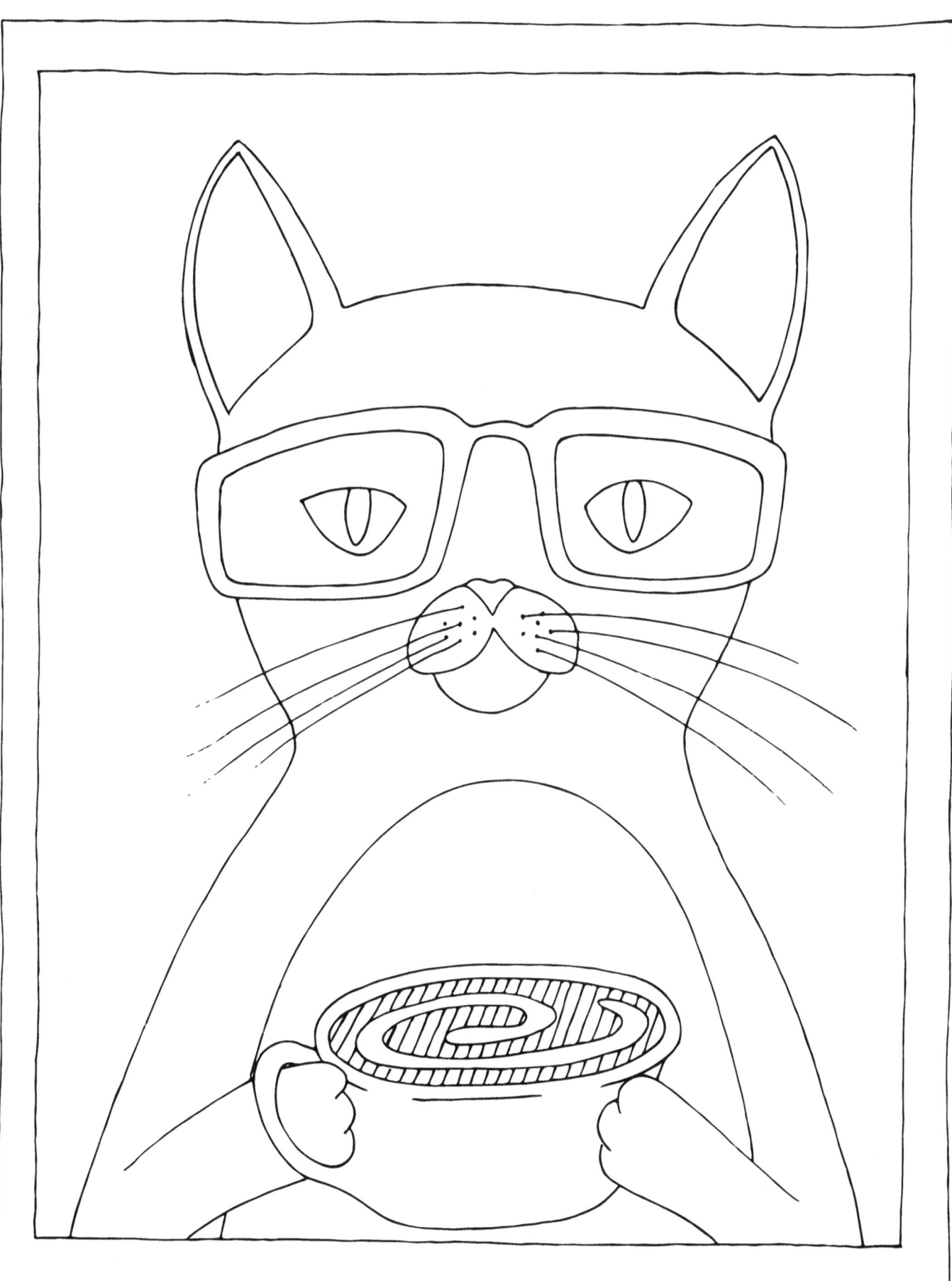